Teamwork:

Working Together,
Accomplishing More

FOUNDED 1870

HV
9469
.H24
1999

ISBN # 1-56991-102-9

About the Authors

Michael D. Maginn is the author of the original manuscript, *Effective Teamwork.*

Adapted for the American Correctional Association by **Ida M. Halasz**, Ph.D., who served as the Deputy Administrator of the National Institute of Corrections Academy, U.S. Department of Justice. Currently, as Vice President of Powell International Inc., she provides training and consulting services to public and private sector organizations.

Foreword

"Teamwork" is probably best known and understood in its relationship to organized sports. However, it also plays an important role in other agencies and organizations, both private and public. Knute Rockne, former Notre Dame football coach, once stated, "The secret of winning football games is working more as a team, less an individual. I don't play my eleven best, but my best eleven." Don't read on until you think about that statement and its meaning. I believe it to be too profound to consider lightly.

What is important about Rockne's statement is that is has relevancy to the athletic arena, a factory, a classroom, and a conference room. Staff must be well trained if they are to accomplish any goal. It is a leader's duty to train staff so that they will be technically proficient and will work as a team. In simple terms, as a team is formed and goals are shared, the end result will show more winners than losers, more success than failure. Production will be up and so will morale.

Obviously, most of the readers of this document will be made up of some part of the Criminal Justice system. So, it is not only important to consider teamwork within our own agency but also to work toward external collaboration because it is difficult to believe that any one group has all of the necessary resources to experience total success on their own.

Teamwork: Working Together, Accomplishing More was developed to assist you in better understanding the teamwork concept and, hopefully, making your professional responsibility a little easier to perform.

Remember, teamwork is the key to accomplishment.

Edward L. Cohn
Commissioner
Indiana Department of Corrections

a publication of the
AMERICAN CORRECTIONAL ASSOCIATION
Professional Development Department
4380 Forbes Boulevard
Lanham, Maryland 20706-4322
(301) 918-1800
Fax: (301) 918-1900
http://www.corrections.com/ACA

Introduction

Thriving on Teams

Teams have a big responsibility. Indeed, members of the team carry a piece of the success of the agency with them. Despite the important role of teams in organizations, however, many people on teams are never taught the skills needed to be team players. That's what this workbook is about—giving people who are on teams fundamental skills, tips, and tactics for being good, effective, contributing team players.

As you work through the following chapters, you will be learning how you can contribute to your team as an effective team player. After completing the exercises and assignments, you should be able to:

- Define what a team is and why a team makes sense for your work unit.

- Identify important team player skills and know how to practice them on your team.

- Evaluate how effective your team is, identifying its strengths and weaknesses.

- Influence your team to develop a sound and useful team code of conduct.

- Contribute your ideas and expertise in solving problems with other team members.

Just as working on a team, this workbook requires your involvement. You may elect to work through it with another team member or on your own. As you read each chapter, you'll find concepts and examples from real work team situations. You will be asked to make choices, judgments, and decisions about various situations. Remember, there are no right or wrong answers in most of these exercises. The idea is to apply basic concepts to various scenarios. In addition, you have the opportunity to do several assignments involving your real work team. Finally, you can use the chapter reviews to help you remember the key points.

As you transfer what you learn from this workbook to real life, you'll find a new level of personal involvement and satisfaction emerging from working with your team. Working on a truly effective team can have a dramatic positive affect on your own productivity. It can also change your view of work and the people you work with.

Table of Contents

Chapter Four

Decisions the Team Can Stand Behind

Chapter Five

Learning to Manage Conflict

Chapter Six

Relax—You'll Love Your New Identity

Self-Assessment

Everyone has been on a team of some kind, whether connected with neighborhood committees, community projects, sports, or other activities. This self-assessment will highlight areas you may want to focus on as you begin to develop team player skills.

Circle True or False in response to the statements below.

1. True/False. The three common traits of a team are shared goals, people having to work together, and a benefit for everyone.

2. True/False. The team should get right down to business and start making decisions as soon as its goals are made clear.

3. True/False. Laughter and silence are two useful and important aspects of a team that is collaborating to solve a serious work problem.

4. True/False. A compromise is better than a consensus.

5. True/False. Conflict on teams is beneficial if members understand how to manage it.

6. True/False. One way to be sure team members arrive at meetings on time is to establish a rule in the team code of conduct.

7. True/False. Making announcements is the most effective use of team meeting time.

8. True/False. When members of a team are committed to a decision, the team has reached a compromise.

9. True/False. Only the members who know the facts should contribute to the solution.

10. True/False. A stakeholder is anyone who is affected by the decisions of a team.

Self-Assessment Answers

1. **True.** A team is any group with common goals, a task that must be done by more than one person, and some kind of benefit for every member.

2. **False.** The team should first develop rules for governing its activities.

3. **True.** Problem solving and creativity inspire both laughter and thought.

4. **False.** Members are committed to consensus decisions. Compromise implies some members are giving up what they want.

5. **True.** Differences among members can be channeled and managed to produce high-quality results.

6. **True.** A team code of conduct is a set of rules that governs the team's activities.

7. **False.** Making announcements, although common in team meetings, is not the best use of meeting time.

8. **False.** A consensus is a decision that team members are committed to.

9. **False.** Anyone involved on a team can be part of the problem-solving process.

10. **True.** A stakeholder may not necessarily be on a team but may be affected by the team's decisions.

Chapter One

What Are Teams All About?

Chapter Objectives

After completing this chapter, you should be able to:

- Define a team and identify common elements in different kinds of teams.

- Describe why working on a team makes sense in your workplace.

- Explain what effective teams do differently than ineffective teams.

- Explore how team player skills help get things done in a team meeting.

- Identify the set of team player skills you need to be an effective team member.

The Team Concept

More organizations of all types and descriptions are creating teams of staff members to get things done. Correctional organizations, law enforcement agencies, manufacturing firms, insurance companies, banks, research labs, hotels, hospitals, service and repair centers, accounting firms, and even restaurants have adopted the team approach. They have combined the talents of separate individuals into a unified group working cooperatively. Why? The results of effective teamwork are impressive. Research shows that people who work in teams:

- Accomplish more on the job with less waste of time and materials.

- Produce higher-quality work.

- Are happier with their jobs.

- Make clients more satisfied—for example, manage offenders more effectively.

Working on a team has definite advantages for you as a staff member, for your correctional organization, and for the offenders. Most people have to learn new interpersonal and process skills to become involved, fully effective, and contributing team players. As you will see, such team player skills help your team work together effectively.

Team player skills are different from those you use every day on the technical part of your job, where you may work on your own. This workbook should help you develop these skills, take an active role on your team, and make a real difference to your work unit and your organization. Let's start with a look at what teams are.

What Is a Team, Anyway?

Good question. You already know the answer. Think about all the kinds of teams you've ever been on or with which you've been involved. Check all the teams with which you're personally familiar.

❑ Sports Teams	❑ Hobby Clubs
❑ Fundraising Groups	❑ Management Teams
❑ Volunteer Organizations	❑ Cross-Functional Teams
❑ Study Groups	❑ Problem-Solving Teams
❑ Employee Committees	❑ Church Groups
❑ Fraternal Orders	❑ Boy Scouts or Girl Scouts
❑ Political Groups	❑ Quality Circles
❑ Work Committees	❑ Boards of Directors
❑ Musical Groups	❑ Chambers of Commerce
❑ School Committees	❑ Industry Associations
❑ Military Units	❑ Labor Union Groups
❑ Work-Unit Teams	❑ Special-Interest Groups
❑ Project Teams	❑ Youth Groups
❑ Parent-Teacher Groups	❑ Speakers Groups

Can you think of any other kinds of teams?

_____

_____

_____

_____

Whatever the label, committee, group, unit, squad, or crew, they're all teams. Do you see what all these teams have in common? These groups share the three following traits.

Team Trait 1: A Shared Purpose or Common Goal

People with different abilities, talents, experience, and backgrounds have come together for a shared purpose or common goal. Whether sharing ideas about fly fishing, planning a work project, or deciding where to hold next year's holiday party, there is a goal everyone is interested in achieving.

What's the common purpose/goal for your work team?

_____

Team Trait 2: People Work Together

All teams' purposes can't be easily achieved, if at all, by people working by themselves. People need other people to achieve the goal. That's another trait of your team.

For example, consider how incredibly difficult it would be to think of new policies and procedures for your work unit by yourself. Then think of how difficult it would be to bring those changes into reality by yourself. How hard would it be without the advice, support, and contribution of other people? Even creative inventors or scientists need other people to help put their ideas to work. Other people bring ideas, expertise, experience, resources, and points of view that are different from yours. Different viewpoints and knowledge mean more brain power is focused on achieving the goal. When all the talent is pooled effectively, no obstacle stands a chance.

Think about the different members on your team. Can you list the unique contribution each person brings to the team?

TEAM MEMBERS	UNIQUE CONTRIBUTION
_____	_____
_____	_____
_____	_____
_____	_____
_____	_____
_____	_____

Team Trait 3: A Benefit for Everyone on the Team

The work of the team—achieving the purpose or the goal—benefits everyone on the team, directly or indirectly. Perhaps everyone's job becomes easier or more satisfying, the organization improves, or each person simply learns something in the process. In teams that function well, members quickly see the benefit to themselves. They become committed to how the team works and the quality of the things the team does.

Not every team starts with a feeling of commitment. Some people feel skeptical about teams because they've never experienced how satisfying a good team can be when working toward a common goal.

Can you think of the benefit(s) to you if your team works effectively and achieves its goal?

_____

_____

_____

When you put together the three traits of a team, you have a good definition of what a team is.

A team is a group of people working together to reach a goal that they all believe in and that would be difficult—if not impossible—to achieve by people working alone.

Are Teams Right for Your Kind of Work?

Here are some reasons why a team approach makes sense for a work unit or organization. Check all that apply to your work unit.

❑ Our correctional supervisors and managers can't possibly make every decision, although they may knock themselves out trying. Work is getting too complex.

❑ The people who do the work have expertise and up-to-date knowledge and know-how about how things really should be done.

❑ Working as individual contributors has been unproductive, communications haven't been good, and conflicts are starting to affect morale. Work is getting hard to do.

❑ There isn't time to wait for someone else to tell us what to do.

❑ Most staff members think they would feel better about work if they had a say in how things get done and if they took responsibility for improving the work outcomes and the work processes.

❑ Staff members in different parts of the organization need to talk to each other more frequently. One group doesn't know what the other is doing.

❑ This correctional organization is changing. We've seen quality improvement programs, staff training, reorganization, and new technology. Teams are the next logical step.

❑ The changing correctional workplace has sent a message to our management that we need to be more creative, more flexible, and more efficient.

❑ We all know the results of our work could be better. We need to continuously improve the quality of our services, reduce cost and waste, and increase all types of security in our organization.

If you're like most people, you've checked at least one, or more likely two or more reasons why a team approach makes sense for you and your work unit. Which of the reasons you checked are the most important and convincing to you?

Important reasons why teams make sense for our organization include:

_____

_____

_____

Chances are, teams are soon going to make a big difference in how you work and how you feel about your work. Most people find that their whole attitude about coming to work changes when they are able to:

- contribute ideas and opinions,
- discuss different ways of doing things, and
- see their team's solutions working effectively.

In fact, members of effective teams even start to feel better about themselves because their co-workers and their organizations value them in new ways.

Another big reason teams make sense is that they give you an opportunity to grow and learn, knowing you have helped make a difference in your organization.

Good Teams and Not-So-Good Teams

Being on a team doesn't guarantee success. Effective teams take work on every member's part. Everyone has to be a team player. Let's look at what being team players can do for a group of people working together toward a common goal.

Take a Moment . . .

You've had experience on teams before. Consider two completely different team experiences you've had. They can be current teams or teams from your past—summer camp, the military, high school, or scouts. Pick one team experience that worked for you. Choose a team that not only accomplished its goal but also did it in a way that left everyone satisfied, even proud of being associated with the team. Pick another team that was a disaster, one you wish you had never joined and that perhaps you even left or from which you resigned. With those two experiences in mind, answer the following questions for each team.

Question	Good Team Experience	Not-So-Good Team Experience
Did members show up on time?		
Did members come prepared?		
Were the meetings organized?		
Did everyone contribute equally?		
Did discussions help the team make decisions?		
What happened when members disagreed?		
Was there more cooperation or more conflict?		
How committed were members to the ideas or decisions made?		
Did people leave feeling good about the team?		
Did members support the team's decisions after the meeting?		

What do you think the difference is between these two teams? You guessed it: on the successful team, individuals were acting like team players. It's not just the team leader. Good team leaders do encourage team members to practice good team player skills. But even the best-trained and most dynamic and fair team leader can't work with a team that is unwilling to contribute, to discuss, and to cooperate. What really counts are the individuals and what they do.

Question	Good Team Experience	Not-So-Good Team Experience
Members arrive on time?	Members are prompt because they know others will be.	Members drift in sporadically, and some leave early.
Members prepared?	Members are prepared and know what to expect.	Members are unclear about what the agenda is.
Members contribute equally?	Members follow a planned agenda.	The agenda is tossed aside, and a free-wheeling discussion ensues.
Discussions help members make decisions?	Members give each other a chance to speak; quiet members are encouraged to contribute.	Some members always dominate the discussion; some are reluctant to speak their minds.
Any disagreement?	Members learn from others' points of view, new facts are discussed, creative ideas evolve, and alternatives emerge.	Members reinforce their belief in their own points of view, or their decisions were made long before the meeting.
More cooperation or more conflict?	Members follow a conflict resolution process established as part of the team's Code of Conduct.	Conflict flares openly, as well as simmers below the surface.
Commitment to decisions?	Cooperation is clearly an important ingredient.	Compromise is the best outcome possible; some members don't care about the result.
Members feelings after team decision?	Members feel satisfied and valued for their ideas.	Members are glad it's over, not sure of results or outcome.
Members support decision afterward?	Members are committed to implementation.	Some members second-guess or undermine the team's decision.

Four Kinds of Team Player Skills

On an effective team, members act differently than those on a less effective team. Many things happen in a team meeting—discussions occur about events and people or what has happened recently or should have happened, opinions are expressed about who should do what, and the like. There are basically four kinds of team player skills that members can use to make a difference and keep their team meetings on track. Known as the "Four C's," these skills are:

1. Team Code of Conduct. Members help develop, follow, and enforce the team's own pre-established policies and procedures—the team's code of conduct. The effective team develops its own rules about how it will conduct its business. These rules range from simple ones, such as having members arrive on time, to complex rules, such as how to resolve conflict.

It is the responsibility of all team members to know and understand these rules and to comply with them for the sake of the team.

2. Team Collaboration. Members discuss ideas and generate alternative and creative solutions. Team members encourage one another to contribute ideas, expand and build on interesting thoughts, and express what is on their minds. When members collaborate on solving a problem, their minds are all working together. The result is often an extraordinarily creative and unique approach to difficult situations.

It is the responsibility of all team members to make sure that everyone gets a chance to offer ideas—even risky or silly-sounding ideas—without being ridiculed or ignored.

A team with consensus is united.

3. Team Consensus. Members make an effort to reach decisions that every team member can support and feel committed to. This not only ensures a team's decisions will be implemented on the job, but it also means members believe the best decision has been made. Consensus is a stronger and more powerful outcome than compromise. A team with consensus is united.

It is the responsibility of team members to stick with a discussion until all issues are unraveled, reservations are resolved, and more positive consensus among members is formed.

4. Team Cooperation in Dealing with Conflict. Instead of turning a disagreement into an emotional argument, members view conflict as a chance to fully explore issues and differences, to discover new data, and to think about decisions from a number of perspectives. Team members don't hide conflict. Effective team members know that conflict is natural. They know that a full, far-reaching, and fact-filled discussion about the conflict will eventually lead members to a clearer understanding of different points of view. Once the underlying problem becomes clear, the resolution is only a few thoughts away.

It is the responsibility of all team members to approach conflict and disagreement nondefensively and to discuss differences open-mindedly. On a team, no one "wins" an argument.

Summary

In this chapter, you learned that a team is a group of people working together to reach a goal that they all believe would be difficult to achieve by people working alone. To be an effective team member, you must:

- follow your team's code of conduct,
- collaborate on ideas and solutions to problems,
- reach a consensus with team members on decisions, and
- cooperate with team members on dealing with conflict.

Chapter One Review

Answers to these questions appear on page 87.

1. List two benefits of working with teams.

   _____

   _____

2. Teams have these traits in common:

   • Share a _____ or _____ goal

   • People _____ together

   • A _____ for everyone on the team

3. List the four C's of team player skills:

   _____

   _____

4. True/False. On a team, the majority wins an argument.

5. True/False. Consensus produces a stronger outcome than compromise.

Chapter Two

Writing the Team Code of Conduct

Chapter Objectives

After completing this chapter, you should be able to:

- Identify the role of a code of conduct in making a team work more effectively.

- Explain the kinds of rules teams can make for themselves.

- Develop a draft team code of conduct.

- Identify ideas from a sample code of conduct that may be useful to you.

- Describe ways that you, as a member, can influence the team to stick by its rules.

The Tale of the Formerly Friendly Tourists

A group of tourists, three married couples from the same hometown, arrived in a faraway city. After settling in, they gathered in the hotel lobby to make an important decision on how to spend their day together seeing the sights.

"That's easy," said one. "Let's go to the art museums and then the cathedral."

"Wait a minute, I'd like to go shopping and then go on a bus tour," said another.

"Okay, I've got it," said a third. "The men can go to their museums and restaurants, and the women can go shopping." A pause. The idea was an obvious and uninspiring solution.

One woman spoke up. "Look, I came here to spend time with my husband. I didn't save up for this vacation to walk around a strange city with women I see every day at home. This was supposed to be our time together. It's important to me."

American Correctional Association

Three of the six folded their arms, bowing out of the conversation. This was not their idea of a vacation. The remaining three juggled ideas. One finally said, "You know, we've made this too difficult, and we're wasting time. Why don't we all go our separate ways and meet for dinner around 7 P.M.?"

"But people eat dinner here at 9 or 10 at night," said another, with an air of frustration.

"So, I'm still going to be hungry by 6 o'clock," said another, arguing against the local dinner hour custom, explaining in detail the nutritional reasons to eat earlier.

By then, the group was tired of discussing where to go and when to meet for dinner. Some of the members knew the next major decision was going to be what restaurant and what to eat. The thought of another negotiation made everyone tense. After all, this city offered many fine choices.

The couples eventually went their own ways. They went out to dinner and spent time together but never as a whole group. Also, there were strained relations and aggrieved feelings about which couple went to dinner with what other couple. Over the next two weeks, tensions grew. When the tourists went home, they were somewhat disappointed with the vacation, and they silently blamed each other.

Ask yourself:

- What went wrong? What would you have done differently?

  _____

  _____

- Have you ever been involved in a situation like this, especially with a new team? If so, what happened?

  _____

  _____

The Importance of a Code of Conduct

A major mistake that teams make, especially new teams, is to plunge right into the team's work (like the decision-making discussion the tourists struggled through) before defining a way to work together. If the hapless tourists had spent a few moments deciding *how* to make the decisions, they probably would have had a much more successful vacation.

At least, they would have remained friends.

Effective teams have a way of avoiding these problems. They take time to decide how to do the things the team has to do, a process called writing the team's code of conduct. The U.S. Constitution describes how our government will work. Similarly, a team's code of conduct establishes operating principles, policies, and ground rules that everyone on the team learns, understands, and is willing to comply with. As the tourists have shown us, if team members don't take time to discuss how to work together, conflict soon sparks and then erupts.

A team's code of conduct establishes ground rules.

Expectations

Let's imagine you've been selected to be on a new work-unit team. You may be pleased, but perhaps, deep down, you feel some reservations.

Can you list any reservations or assumptions you would have about what the team experience will be like?

_____

_____

_____

_____

_____

Most people working on a team for the first time feel a little tentative about what will happen on the team and their role on it. These feelings are a natural response to the situation. Check off any unspoken expressions and assumptions you may have. Be honest in your answers.

- ❑ I'm not going to contribute anything unless someone asks me a direct question.

- ❑ I'm not sure what this team is supposed to do.

- ❑ The loudest voice is going to get his or her way.

- ❑ If I can't bring up whatever is on my mind, I'm not convinced this team is going to work.

- ❑ This team will probably start with a lot of interest and commitment but, by the third or fourth meeting, that will drop off or be gone.

- ❑ One or two people will eventually do all the work. Every group has a couple of workhorses who volunteer for tasks and/or carry the load.

- ❑ If all I have to do is talk, that's all right. I'm too busy to do anything else for this team.

- ❑ What will I have to do to get the team doing what I know is right?

- ❑ I wonder which person will dominate the discussions.

- ❑ This is going to take a lot of time, in fact, forever.

- ❑ I can miss a couple of meetings. It's okay.

- ❑ When will my commitment to the team end?

Ask yourself what happens to teams if these assumptions and expectations come true in team meetings:

_____

_____

Members bring reservations and assumptions to their new team. If these feelings are not addressed, they can lead to fragmentation and difficulties in sustaining commitment to the team. Often, these assumptions are based on past experiences with less-effective teams, whose members didn't practice good team skills. A team code of conduct is designed to clear doubts about what will happen on the team. It creates a positive, specific framework that describes how the team will work—a framework that everyone agrees to follow.

How Does the Team Write a Code of Conduct?

The answer depends on the team. A wise leader will ask for the members' help in identifying the kinds of rules that make sense for the team. The leader then will work with the team to develop and document the rules before they are needed. A less desirable procedure is to wait until problems occur, signaling that the team needs policies and standard practices. Next, we'll look at two ways to write a team code of conduct.

Method One: Future-Forward— The Team Victory Party

One way to approach the task of writing a team code of conduct is to imagine the future success of the team. Then, work backward from there, defining what it took to get there. Let's say you're starting a major team project. Ask yourself and the other members to imagine that the project has been completed successfully and effectively.

From this future perspective, amidst the (future) good feelings and celebration, look back and ask:

- ❑ What were our meetings like? How were they conducted?

- ❑ How did we reach high-quality decisions?

- ❑ Who was involved and when?

- ❑ What indicators told us we were doing a good job as a team?

- ❑ How did people feel about being on the team? Why did they feel that way?

- ❑ How were crises and problems handled? What was the atmosphere in the meeting room?

- ❑ How were differences of opinion handled? How did people feel about discussions?

- ❑ What role did the team leader play?

Think through the answers to these questions. For example, how did people feel about being on the team? On an effective team, members will practice good team skills. The members will feel valued, glad they have a chance to contribute, and proud to be associated with the group. Now, what did the team do to ensure that people would feel valued? In team meetings, people respected other members' feelings. That's a team rule: Respect the feelings of others.

What indicators told us we were doing a good job as a team? There were probably lots of indicators. We want those that were important to our team. An indicator could be the number of times we sat down and asked ourselves how effective our team was and got any team issues on the table. That's a potential team rule: Sit down regularly and discuss how we're doing.

Take a Moment . . .

Take a minute to "think forward" to your team's party. Can you list the kinds of rules in your team's code of conduct that got you there?

_____

_____

Method Two: Anticipating Predictable Problems

Another way to develop a team code of conduct is to examine the list of predictable and frequent problems any team can expect—especially in its early stages. The team's task is to come up with ideas to avoid these problems, ideas everyone can agree with, ideas that are tailored to your own situation.

Here is a list of some typical team problems. You can probably add your own. See what policies and rules you can put in your code of conduct to head off these problems before they get in the way of team effectiveness.

Predictable Problem: Important People Not Included

Staff members who should have been involved with the team from the beginning weren't, leading to problems in selling or implementing the team's decisions. The problem is that the team doesn't discover this omission until important decisions requiring the buy-in of other people have already been made. What rules can be established to make sure that the right people are involved? (Hint: Identify everyone who will be involved with the results or outcomes of the team's work.)

_____

_____

_____

_____

_____

Predictable Problem: Undisciplined Behavior at Team Meetings

Members arrive late or not at all. Those who do come are unprepared. Some leave early, some get up to take or make phone calls, some read or work on other projects. Noisy private conversations interrupt discussion. Even worse, deadlines and commitments are not met. Apparently, some members don't take the work of the team seriously.

What rules can be established to ensure that the team meetings are disciplined and uphold respect for individuals? (Hint: What about a clear statement of expectations?)

_____

_____

_____

_____

_____

_____

_____

_____

_____

_____

_____

_____

_____

Predictable Problem: Long, Drawn-Out Discussions

Discussion is central to how a team works. Some lengthy discussions are necessary when making a complex decision. On the other hand, when these discussions are unproductive and rambling, time is wasted. People become disinterested and eventually agree to anything simply to get out of the meeting. What rules can help keep discussions to the point and productive? (Hint: Consider adopting a meeting format, such as old business, new business, other business or problem statement, ideas, solution choices, and final selection.)

_____

_____

_____

_____

_____

_____

_____

_____

_____

_____

_____

_____

_____

_____

Predictable Problem: Complaining

Some members think the team meeting is a place to complain about everything they don't like about work. Team meetings encourage participation. However, the focus of the team's work is to develop solutions, not to dwell on how individual team members are affected by problems.

What rules can be established to discourage members from using the meeting as their outlet to complain about work or other staff members? (Hint: Doesn't every team have a goal? What's your team's goal? Doesn't everyone—even a member with complaints—have positive ideas about how to improve things?)

_____

_____

_____

_____

_____

_____

_____

_____

_____

_____

_____

_____

Predictable Problem: The Dominating Team Member

Every team has one or two members who talk the most or who simply don't give other members time to finish what they're saying. While these staff members may have good ideas, other members don't feel good about the process because discussion seems closed to them. What can your team do to control those who tend to dominate discussions, without offending them or turning off their ideas? (Hint: Isn't there a way to encourage equal participation?)

_____

_____

_____

_____

_____

_____

_____

_____

_____

_____

_____

_____

_____

_____

_____

_____

_____

Consider your work team and some of the problems you've been facing. Looking over these problems, can you identify some rules that may help avoid or eliminate these problems in the future?

_____

_____

_____

_____

_____

_____

_____

_____

_____

In case you haven't noticed, you've just drafted a team code of conduct through these different methods. Compare your ideas with the sample on the next page. Note any ideas you feel will be useful to your own team.

_____

_____

_____

_____

_____

_____

_____

_____

Our Team's Code of Conduct

We will always be on time for meetings. Right on time. If we must be late or absent, we will inform the team leader or a team member at least a day in advance.

We will always come to meetings prepared to work on the agenda that we will receive before the meeting. Our preparation and data collection will be complete, and we will be ready to discuss the issues on the agenda.

We will always respect the opinions and feelings of all individuals. Each member has equal participation in our meetings. When discussing team business, members should expect to contribute to discussions and be listened to with respect.

We will always avoid blaming people for the shortcomings of our team. If our team somehow fails to do its tasks properly, we will examine our team process and attempt to improve it. If individuals are having trouble meeting their commitments, the team will support them in every way possible.

Members will support the decisions of the team after they are made. Undermining team decisions or second-guessing and bad-mouthing the team and its work outside the team setting to non-members is unacceptable behavior.

Members will live up to their team commitments, recognizing that failure to do so affects the whole team's progress. When in jeopardy of not meeting their obligations, members will notify the team in time for other members to take supportive action.

When faced with a decision, we will first decide how to make the decision. Our general rule is to (1) state the problem, (2) discuss different ideas, (3) examine the benefits and risks associated with different approaches, and (4) select an approach we can all support. Other methods may be appropriate.

We will deal with conflict in a productive way. Our general rule for conflict is to understand the problem as best we can from each side's perspective. To do that, we will listen to all sides of the conflict, looking for facts and evidence. If there is still a conflict about facts, we will gather additional data. When the problem is understood, the team will help those in conflict create alternative approaches. If misunderstandings are not corrected through this approach, we will call a special meeting to address the conflict.

We recognize that working on a team usually results in high-quality ideas and decisions, as well as fun. If we find we are not experiencing these benefits of teamwork, we will pause to assess how we are working together and to better understand our team and our work.

Ten Ways a Team Member Can Influence the Team Code of Conduct

Even if you're not the team leader, you can still play a role in developing and enforcing the team's rules. Check the ideas that make sense to you:

- ❑ Ask members if they are satisfied with how the team is operating. Suggest an examination of the team process.

- ❑ When a team crisis occurs, take a step back from the problem and examine what kind of problem it is, then determine how you can solve it and prevent it from happening again.

- ❑ Make sure that everyone on the team—especially new members— knows and understands the rules in the team's code of conduct.

- ❑ Diplomatically—and privately—suggest to persistent violators of the code of conduct that they should examine their degree of commitment to the team.

- ❑ Ask other teams how they manage their process, make decisions, and resolve conflict. Use their successful methods for your own team.

- ❑ Publicize your team's success, based on the team code of conduct. Make sure that everyone in the organization knows and appreciates the effectiveness of your team's ideas for self-governance.

- ❑ Review the code of conduct before critical meetings that require consensus or collaboration.

- ❑ Don't be shy or reluctant to speak. When you see a violation of the code of conduct, speak up. It's your team and your code of conduct.

- ❑ Ask the team to form a committee whose goal is to monitor compliance with the code of conduct.

- ❑ Ask the team to review the code of conduct from time to time to be sure that it is still relevant to the work of the team.

Summary

In this chapter, you learned about the importance of teams developing a code of conduct. This code establishes how the team will work together—its operating principles, policies and ground rules that all team members learn, understand and are willing to comply with.

The two methods for writing a code of conduct are

1) future forward, and

2) anticipating predictable problems.

Chapter Two Review

Answers to these questions appear on page 87.

1. Define the term "code of conduct."

   _____

   _____

   _____

   _____

   _____

2. List two benefits of a code of conduct.

   _____

   _____

3. Describe the future-forward method of writing a code of conduct.

   _____

   _____

   _____

   _____

4. Describe the "anticipating predictable problems" method of writing a code of conduct.

    _____

    _____

    _____

    _____

    _____

5. You can influence your team's code of conduct by:

    *   Asking other _____ how they manage their process,

    *   Not being ____ __ _____ ___ _____,

    *   Asking the team to _____ the code of conduct from time to time,

    *   Reviewing the code of conduct before _____ _____ that require consensus or collaboration, and

    *   Asking the team to form a committee whose goal is to _____ _____ with the code of conduct.

Chapter Three

How to Get Ideas on the Table

Chapter Objectives

After completing this chapter, you should be able to:

- Describe what team collaboration is.
- Identify what helps and hinders the creative process.
- List the actions a team member can use in collaborating with other team members.
- Describe how to apply team collaboration skills to different problems.

Collaboration

Solving a problem as a group is different from solving a problem as an individual. The team has the power of different ideas and points of view. When team members collaborate effectively, ideas from different people produce creative alternatives and unique approaches to stubborn problems.

What's it like to work on a team that enjoys creating as many alternative solutions as possible? It's fun! That's why team collaboration is the most playful and creative team skill. In this chapter, we'll explore how team members can open the door to solving problems together.

A Collaboration Sampler

Try this exercise by yourself.

Take 60 seconds to list as many uses for a marshmallow as you can. Have fun, be unorthodox. Write in the space below:

_____

_____

_____

_____

_____

How many? Now ask three other people to list as many uses for a marshmallow as the group can in 60 seconds. Add their uses for a marshmallow:

_____

_____

_____

_____

_____

A team has the wisdom, experience, diversity, and creativity of its members.

As you can see, it's more fun and productive to do these tasks in teams. Not only are there more ideas, some of them are really bizarre. You see, teamwork has a distinct advantage. A team has the wisdom, experience, diversity, and creativity of its members. Once a team has a clear and useful code of conduct as a foundation, they can collaborate on addressing problems.

What emerges from team collaboration? Insightful, perhaps even startlingly high-quality ideas and decisions to improve work, to design new policies or procedures, or simply to remove stubborn problems that get in the way of work.

The key to collaboration is to open the door to ideas, and team members have that key in their possession. Members have a responsibility to create an environment in which ideas can be discussed freely. Teams that collaborate well allow members to have different and unusual ideas with no threat of embarrassment or disapproval. Team members build on each other's ideas, modify them, drop them, and pick them up again—a volleyball game of thoughts.

What Slows Down Collaboration?

People have good ideas, sometimes creative and unusual ideas, all the time. Yes, you're creative. You may not think so, but everyone is. Creativity doesn't mean only being artistic or expressive. We learn as children to play in imaginary worlds where ideas flow and anything is possible. When we grow up, we learn to become sensitive, sometimes overly sensitive, to what other people think of our ideas. We learn to keep these ideas and images inside. Our thoughts often go unexpressed, especially in team settings. We are afraid that ideas that were once playful and full of potential might be viewed by others as silly and unbusinesslike.

Paradoxically, organizations need ideas that are different. Where would the great inventions and innovations of today be if the ideas behind them had been put down when they were first expressed? Isn't it silly to think of delivering packages and small parcels overnight by using a huge fleet of airplanes and trucks? Ten years ago, wasn't it comical to think of sending letters over the telephone? Can you think of other everyday inventions that were developed from different, innovative ideas?

_____

_____

_____

_____

_____

_____

_____

Credit cards, self-service gas stations, telephone answering machines, mail-order flowers, television remote controls, frequent flyer clubs, the list goes on. How about some of the great ideas that have emerged in corrections. List a few that your agency or facility uses.

_____

_____

Even more ideas would come to light within a supportive team atmosphere.

Imagine the first meeting in which someone said, "Let's consider putting devices on nonviolent offenders to track them in the community, rather than keeping them locked up." That team meeting must have been interesting! But it's not always that simple. It's too easy to stop ideas cold just because they haven't been done already.

How to Stop Ideas Cold

Check off the expressions you've heard in team meetings. How do you think the members offering the ideas felt?

- ❑ We tried that already, and it didn't work.

- ❑ Are you serious? Come on!

- ❑ Are you kidding? Come on!

- ❑ Oh sure, the taxpayers will buy that idea!

- ❑ They'll never buy that.

- ❑ That's not what we had in mind. (Someone has preconceived ideas of the solution.)

- ❑ Nice thought. Any other ideas? (Whoops, your idea got swept away.)

- ❑ I'm not sure you know enough about it. (Ideas are limited to areas of expertise.)

- ❑ You're not suggesting we do that, are you?

- ❑ We'll never make it work.

- ❑ It won't last.

- ❑ The public will never support a crazy idea like that.

- ❑ It'll cost too much.

- ❑ Can't we be logical?

- ❑ Yes, but . . .

How to Bring Ideas to Life

Team members can control the creative atmosphere in meetings. When members practice collaboration skills, everyone is encouraged to offer suggestions. The more suggestions, the more likely the team will come up with new and effective approaches to stubborn problems.

What To Do and *How* To Do It

1. **Listen with interest and respect what members say.**

    Use positive body language (lean forward, take notes). Demonstrate active listening skills (say, "Uh-huh, I see," and repeat important phrases) to let members know you're tuned in and attentive. Allow members to complete their statements without interruption or distractions.

2. **Pursue what is interesting about unique and different ideas.**

    Find the best trait of the idea being offered. For example, "Reducing the amount of information on the form is really interesting."

    Build on ideas by repeating the unique trait and support or expand it. "Less information means a person would complete the form right away from memory." Encourage the member offering the idea to keep explaining what's on his/her mind. "Stick with it, Joan. Tell us more." Ask follow-up questions.

3. **Acknowledge and record every idea as it comes up.**

    Use a flip chart or chalkboard to list ideas. All team members should acknowledge contributions. "Way to go, Chris! Nice idea."

4. **Ask others to go beyond the obvious.**

    Encourage team members to stretch their imaginations. "Come on, team, we need a breakthrough idea." Ask the team to do a loosening up exercise, like collecting uses for a marshmallow. Give people permission to be creative. Remember, the first solution is not necessarily the best solution.

5. **Collect a quantity of ideas.**

    Quality will soon become evident. Ask members to state as many ideas as possible. The team will have time to refine them later. Keep asking, "Any other ideas?" and wait until they emerge. Stick with it. Don't be discouraged if ideas develop slowly.

6. **Allow time for thinking.**

    Don't confuse silence with inattentiveness. Silence is the sound of thinking. Change the meeting location. Take a break or walk.

Come back tomorrow. Change the subject. Ignore periods of confusion and frustration. They're natural.

7. **Ask critics for ideas and suggestions.**

If someone criticizes an idea, ask him/her to offer new ideas in its place or build on the idea in question.

8. **Encourage people to ask "what if" questions.**

Use a metaphor. "What if our application form were on a postcard? What information would we ask for?" Remove constraints. "What if we did have time to solve this problem? What would the solution look like?" Change perceptions. "What if Joe Q. Citizen were solving this problem? What would he or she say?" Draw the problem as a picture.

9. **Avoid criticism and judgment of ideas.**

Advise naysayers about the team code of conduct. Treat all ideas equally as they are expressed. Reward people for their contributions.

10. **Have fun.**

Order pizza. If possible in your organization, wear casual clothes, sit on the floor, close the door, play music. Give everyone a kazoo. (It's been done in the best of correctional organizations!) The relaxed atmosphere will help members generate creative ideas.

Which of these skills is your team already fairly good at?

_____

_____

_____

_____

Which need improvement?

_____

_____

_____

_____

Take a Moment . . .

Team Collaboration Exercises:
Get Ready for Creativity

You'll need to work with at least two team members. Before you begin an exercise, select one or two team collaboration skills to practice during the exercise. Watch the interaction among team members as you develop your ideas.

1. On a flip chart, draw a new logo for your correctional organization. Make sure that it reflects what people really value and think.

2. Can you identify 100 no-cost ways to improve quality in your work unit? How about 50?

3. Imagine your team has invented a machine that makes nonliving objects weightless. Develop an advertisement for the product, including its name, slogans, and features and benefits. Draw your advertisement on a flip chart.

4. Remember the Mona Lisa, one of Leonardo da Vinci's masterpieces? Can you and your friends explain the real story behind the smiling face? Write down all the possible explanations.

5. Gather some old magazines and cut out pictures. A medium-sized stack will do. Now, with your friends, put the pictures together in a sequence to tell a story that somehow ends with you and your colleagues. When you're ready, tell the story to your team.

Tips for Improving Team Collaboration Skills

If you and your team worked through some of the exercises and applied the team collaboration skills, you probably laughed a lot. But perhaps more important, you probably created more interesting results than you could have by yourselves. **By doing creative warm-up exercises at every team meeting, members will soon get the idea that problem solving is fun**. Here are some additional suggestions for making team collaboration work. Check those that you want to take back to your team.

❑ **Practice, practice, practice** is the best way to improve team members' collaboration skills.

❑ Most people need permission to let their ideas out. **Tell them it's okay to offer interesting,** even unorthodox or different, ideas.

❑ **Post team collaboration skills on the wall and review them before the next meeting.**

❑ **Allow time for ideas to happen.** A problem can be so difficult or complex that original thoughts need to incubate, perhaps over a few hours or overnight. When members' enthusiasm for problem solving seems to fade, the team should take a break.

❑ **Suggest that your team visit other teams that are good at collaboration skills.** Ask members to come to your meetings. Compare the creative process in both groups and learn from each other.

❑ **Get an outside facilitator to attend your meetings.** Having an outsider act as a referee and facilitator is a highly effective way to explore the barriers to creativity on your team.

❑ **Ask your team to practice "ambiance engineering."** Change the meeting room around. Move furniture, meet in the staff lunch room, meet off site, meet outside, wear different clothes, play a game, and do the unexpected.

❑ **Study the problem.** Do some action research. Visit the problem where it happens. Observe how the problem occurs, talk to the people actually involved, perform any tasks or operations yourself, experience what it's like to be a recipient of the problem.

❑ **Celebrate an exciting and productive team meeting with a fun event outside of work.** Go to a movie or on a boat ride. Show a Charlie Chaplin movie.

❑ **Think of some respected and credible figure in your organization or the criminal justice field**—a person who has a good reputation for creativity, ideas, and uniqueness. **Ask the team to think about how that person would address the problem.**

Summary

In this chapter, you learned about collaboration or group problem solving. Of all the team skills, collaboration is clearly the most fun. When members collaborate, they identify innovative and ingenious ways to solve problems. To ensure effective collaboration, remember to:

- Not allow your preconceptions to color your view of teammates' capabilities. (Everyone can be creative.)

- Give permission to everybody to be creative in an effort to solve problems.

- Allow plenty of time for idea development.

- Never dismiss an idea for seeming silly or frivolous. These are opportunities to develop new approaches.

- Listen to all ideas.

- Encourage teammates to play with concepts and ideas even before a serious idea emerges.

- Perhaps break up heavy sessions with less serious activities to ease tension and change the pace. After a tension-reducing break, you can go back to the problem with renewed energy.

Chapter Three Review

Answers to these questions appear on page 88.

1. What is collaboration?

   _____

   _____

   _____

   _____

2. Collaboration is slowed down by team members':

   ___ A. Hidden agendas
   ___ B. Anger
   ___ C. Personality traits
   ___ D. Fear

3. True/False. Team members can control the creative atmosphere in meetings.

4. List three ways to help bring creative ideas to the table.

   _____

   _____

   _____

5. List two ways to improve team collaboration skills.

   _____

   _____

Chapter Four

Decisions the Team Can Stand Behind

Chapter Objectives

After completing this chapter, you should be able to:

- Distinguish between consensus and compromise.

- Identify the benefits of consensus in team decision making.

- Identify the kinds of decisions that will benefit from decision making by consensus.

- Identify the team consensus skills you can use in your team.

- Describe how to apply team consensus skills in an exercise.

Problem: Five team members have to agree on selecting a new member. Before they discuss the candidates, the members decide to identify the selection criteria. They agree on three qualities the new member should have—technical expertise, willingness to participate, and cooperativeness. They are having trouble deciding on the fourth, and final, criterion.

"I say it's loyalty," said the first member. "If people aren't loyal to the team, they can undo all our decisions after we make them."

The second member responded, "Loyalty? Isn't that a bit old-fashioned? It sounds like conformity to me. We need people who can think independently and have ideas, not loyal dull heads."

The first member replied, "Who says people who are loyal have to be dull or nonthinking?"

"Well, that's what comes to my mind," the second member rejoined.

The discussion went around the table. The other members gave their views of loyalty. To one, loyalty meant standing up for the team whenever it was challenged by others, defending its decisions. To another, loyalty meant following the team's code of conduct and being a team player—sticking to the rules and doing an equal share. To the next person, loyalty was more practical.

"To me, loyalty means agreeing to follow the team's direction, even though you originally thought it was incorrect."

"Well," said the first team member, "I guess that really focuses the difference on me. My idea of loyalty—being a conformist—doesn't seem to be the same. You two think a person who is loyal is a good soldier, someone who does what he or she is told."

The team discussed these differences. The member who had viewed loyalty as conformity agreed that the others' views made sense, but he still had trouble with the word loyalty.

"If loyalty means different things to this group, it'll have all kinds of different meanings to our candidates," he said.

The team agreed on the term "team player" to incorporate all their thoughts about loyalty, and each one felt committed to the decision.

The four selection criteria were then used to identify many excellent candidates. The next consensus the group faced was selecting the candidate who best matched the criteria. It was difficult, but they emerged with a person they all agreed upon. And they all felt she was the right choice.

Let's take a look at this situation. What does the word loyalty mean to you? What would you have said in the team meeting? Would you have agreed with the consensus? Think it over and then write down your answers.

_____

_____

_____

_____

_____

_____

This team reached consensus by exchanging views about the meaning of a particular word. When each member expressed what the word meant to him or her, the team was able to see similarities and differences. When members discussed differences in an open-minded way, the team was able to agree on what they really meant. The team came to a decision they could all stand behind.

We're going to explore the concept of team consensus and what you, as a member, can do to influence consensus decisions on a team.

Compromise vs. Consensus

You and some friends are going to rent a movie one evening. Everyone wants a different one. Some of the group—but not you—feel rather strongly about certain films and movie stars. Do you:

- Dig your heels in and defend your choice?

- Pick up a book and read in another room?

- Go along with what people want?

In this kind of situation, you probably would just go along with whatever movie was selected. You don't care much about the movie anyway. It's probably more important and fun just being with your friends than winning the movie argument. This is an example of a compromise decision. What words do you associate with compromise? What about the consequences of a compromise decision?

_____

_____

_____

Compromise

A compromise is a way of getting a decision people can live with. Generally, the result is all right but not terrific. Some words that you might associate with a compromise might be halfhearted, reluctant, settlement, concession, or arrangement. Some people say that a camel is an animal designed by the compromises of a committee.

Certainly, compromises are important and expedient answers to some problems. The problem with a compromise is that the outcome doesn't meet everyone's expectations. In fact, there may be some winners and losers in a compromise decision. When people make a decision they are not 100 percent committed to, they may feel halfhearted and reluctant about putting that decision into action.

Can you think of any decisions your team may have made that were compromises? How did members feel about this? Write a description of your reaction to a real compromise decision.

_____

_____

_____

_____

Consensus—Making a Lasting Decision

Your work team has been asked to decide if the probation office should adopt flexible work-hour scheduling. Staff would have to work 40 hours a week. But individuals could work four 10-hour days, or one 12-hour day and four 7-hour days, or other combinations of time—as long as it resulted in a full 40 hours. As you can see, there are some obvious advantages as well as disadvantages. Management needs your team's decision in two hours. Do you:

1. Fold your arms and watch the argument unfold?

2. Argue forcefully for your optimal time slot?

3. Discuss what people think and see how the group feels?

4. Decide the decision is too complex to make, so you recommend saying no to flexible scheduling?

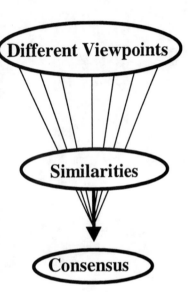

Opting out of making decisions because they appear complex or difficult is not a good idea. It only means that opportunities for improving work and the quality of work life will slip by. Or, even worse, the decisions may be made by someone else. Arguing on the basis of self-interest will lead only to more arguing, delaying a decision until individuals are worn down and willing to compromise, and you now know where that leads.

This decision requires a group commitment. That kind of agreement is called a consensus. Basically the process of achieving consensus involves getting people with different points of view to start seeing things in a similar way or at least narrowing their differences.

A Story:

The King, the Three Wise People, and the Mysterious Animal

A rich king was intrigued by reports of an unusual animal that lived far across the sea. He decided to send his three brightest and wisest scholars to visit the animal and bring back a description. The three traveled to the far-off land, finally arriving at night at the edge of a dense jungle, where they heard the animal thrashing around in a grove of trees. In the pitch-black darkness, each of the wise people—quite afraid by now—walked into the grove to touch the animal. One by one they emerged, and they quickly departed to report to the king.

Back at the castle, the king asked eagerly, "What is this animal like?" "Why, it had a great side as far up as I could reach," said the first wise person. "No, it was thin and had a hairy head," said the second. "No, no, it had a thick round neck," said the third. The three began arguing about what the animal was like. Each had touched the same animal, but how could they see it so differently? The king, thinking of the expenses of sending three so-called wise people on such a long trip, had them all thrown into the dungeon. He still didn't know what the mysterious animal looked like.

Unfortunately, the wise people never shared their points of view, their perceptions. To each one, his or her own view of the elephant was the only correct one.

Consensus brings team members to a common understanding of the issues.

In a consensus, the various points of view of each member of the team are considered, discussed, compared, and discussed again—until everyone sees all parts of the elephant. Members begin to learn about others' perceptions, and a decision or approach emerges as differences are understood and narrowed. This outcome goes beyond something people can go along with. Instead, it is a decision team members believe in as the truly best way to go, given the circumstances. The issue has been examined, re-examined, tested through discussion, critiqued, poked, and prodded. Thus, all members of the team can see the problem and the solutions from many different points of view.

One of the major benefits of a consensus decision is that it brings team members (who start off with differing points of view) to a common understanding of all the issues. In a way, it's a learning experience. Members learn how others see their part of the elephant. Through discussion of how fellow members see the problem, everyone begins to share perceptions. Differences don't appear as great as they once did.

Building a Shared View—10 Consensus Skills

Team members can practice consensus skills any time the group needs to reach a decision that everyone must buy into. When the decision is actually implemented in the work unit, people support it and the desired results start to happen. Here are a few ways to narrow differences in points of view among team members.

What to Do and *How* to Do It

1. **Ask each individual how he or she feels about the situation and why.**

   Go around the table and give everyone his or her say. "How do you see this problem, Pat?" Stop the team members who are dominating the discussion and poll everyone else. Ask members who are silent what they think.

2. **Ask for facts, definitions, or explanations, and try to uncover what different thoughts or words really mean to team members.**

   Ask members to explain their views. Focus on words. For instance, "What does safe mean to you?" or "What's a significant delay?" Ask, "How do you know that?" when faced with questionable statements.

3. **Clarify discrepancies of opinion with fact.**

State facts and ask other team members to compare their opinions with the facts. Ask members to support competing points of view with facts. If there are no available facts, ask members to gather data before continuing.

4. **Modify your views when faced with compelling facts.**

Listen to the facts underlying differing points of view. Test the facts being presented against your viewpoint. Weigh the effect on you and the team of continuing to resist ideas in the face of convincing facts. Try on the other point of view and see how it feels. Is it really that different from yours? Are the consequences acceptable?

5. **Identify similarities and differences among the points of view in the team.**

Make a list of similarities on a flip chart or chalkboard. Ask different members to state what is similar about their ideas. Crystallize the differences among the team members in a simple statement, "It seems some people view centralization as a threat, while others see it as an opportunity."

6. **Reinforce open-mindedness—that is, the willingness to listen to other views—and the need for cooperation.**

Remind members about the team code of conduct concerning open discussion. Give people time to talk. Make sure that they have said what is on their minds. Review the team's goal from time to time, and stress the need to work together to come to an agreement.

7. **Remain nondefensive when challenged and avoid emotional encounters.**

Stay silent and calm when being criticized. Wait until the other member has finished before commenting. Take notes reflecting the other member's points. Summarize the other member's opinion in your own words. If the meeting is getting emotional, ask for a short recess, take a walk, try to relax. Be empathic with the other member's views. Say, "I can understand why you would say that."

8. **List the positive and negative aspects or consequences of each point of view.**

   Assume the team has adopted a particular viewpoint. Ask the members to discuss the advantages and disadvantages. Repeat the process with the next opinion. Explore the risks associated with each idea. Test how realistic the risks are. For example, "Will we really have more complaints from inmates?"

9. **Be sure that each team member participates.**

   Go around the table and ask all the members what they think. "What do you think loyalty means?" Members have a right to speak their minds.

10. **Through discussion, define the risk level associated with a decision not working and develop an approach that minimizes that risk for everyone.**

    Ask people what concerns them about a specific course of action. "What do you think will happen if we make the changes in the visitation schedule?" If concerns are based on misperception or misunderstanding, explain the facts. "Gary, the change is on Sunday only. Does that clear things up?" Balance the advantages and risks of each approach. Ask the team what level of risk it is willing to accept. We're talking about risk in the general sense of whether the decision will work—not in the sense of physical safety.

Take a Moment . . .

Before going on, ask yourself how well your team practices these consensus skills. Rate each skill from 1 to 5 according to the following scale. Identify which skills need improvement and, in the space provided, list some ideas for improving that skill among your team members.

Do We:	Rarely	Not Usually	Some- times	Most of the Time	Always
1. Ask each individual how he or she feels about the situation and why?	1	2	3	4	5
2. Ask for facts or explanations, and try to uncover what different thoughts or words mean to everyone?	1	2	3	4	5
3. Clarify discrepancies of opinions with facts?	1	2	3	4	5
4. Modify our views when faced with compelling facts and opinions?	1	2	3	4	5
5. Identify similarities and differences among the points of view on the team?	1	2	3	4	5
6. Reinforce open-mindedness—the willingness to listen to other views—and the need for cooperation?	1	2	3	4	5
7. Remain nondefensive when challenged, and avoid emotional encounters?	1	2	3	4	5
8. List the positive and negative aspects or consequences of each point of view?	1	2	3	4	5
9. Make sure that each team member participates?	1	2	3	4	5
10. Define the risk level associated with a decision not working and develop an approach that minimizes the risk for everyone?	1	2	3	4	5

What are your team members' three highest-rated skills? What are members doing in team meetings to earn that score?

Three Highest-Rated Skills   **Actions**

_____   _____

_____   _____

_____   _____

Now, identify the three lowest-rated skills of team members. Identify things you and your team can do to improve these consensus skills. Refer to the "How to Do It" suggestions.

Three Lowest-Rated Skills   **Improvement Ideas**

_____   _____

_____   _____

_____   _____

Team Consensus Exercises—Just Doing It

One way to help your team improve is to work together on a non-work-related problem. While the team is working through the following exercises, each member should try to concentrate on practicing at least one of the team consensus skills. After the exercise is over, ask the team to reflect on how the consensus process went and how well the team consensus skills were applied. Here are several exercises from which to choose.

Team Consensus Exercise 1—Scoring your team's consensus skills (Estimated time: 30 minutes). Each team member has to select at least one team consensus skill before you begin and actively try to practice it during the exercise. After the group has completed the exercise, see how the members felt about the consensus process. Finally, compare this exercise with what really goes on in the team meetings.

Review the list of team consensus skills with your team. Next, have each member rate each skill individually. When everyone is finished, compare the individual ratings and come to agreement on a group rating for each skill. This will require all team members to explain why they gave each rating.

Team Consensus Exercise 2—Lively discussions on hot topics (Estimated time: 30-60 minutes). In this exercise, your team can address several interesting and controversial issues. The idea is for the team to come to a consensus on how it feels. Once again, ask each team member to select a team consensus skill and apply it during the exercise. Here are some issues to discuss. Select one you think would lead to a lively discussion.

1. Vehicular traffic in cities should be limited to delivery trucks and taxis during work hours.

2. Children should be required to do at least one hour of homework every night.

3. Television programs showing violence should be shown only after 9 P.M.

4. Surplus military clothing should be given to the homeless.

5. All correctional staff, including clerical central office staff, must demonstrate proficiency with two types of guns to retain their jobs.

6. Schools should operate year-round, with summer outdoor programs appropriate to the locality.

7. Performance appraisals of team members should reflect the outcomes of the team, not the individuals' accomplishments.

Team Consensus Exercise 3—The excellent team member (Estimated time: 45 minutes). Before the team exercise begins, ask each member to select a team consensus skill and apply it in the consensus process. Have your team review the following list of 20 descriptive words. Each team member is to select only five words that, according to him or her, describe the most important traits of a team member. After members have made their individual choices, the team has to arrive at a consensus on the five most important traits of a team member. Which five descriptives will the team choose? Don't vote. Discuss. There are no right or wrong answers to this exercise.

Traits of the Excellent Team Member

1. Speaks up	11. Knowledgeable
2. Experienced	12. Good Thinker
3. Creative	13. Helpful
4. Ambitious	14. Expert
5. Risk Taker	15. Good Networker
6. Motivated	16. Efficient
7. Respected	17. A Leader
8. Sensitive	18. People Person
9. Interesting	19. Energetic
10. Willing	20. Well Known

Summary

In this chapter, you learned about the benefits of consensus. Consensus is the agreement and commitment of the team to an idea or decision. Consensus building is one of the most powerful team-player skills. Members who reach consensus find that decisions are implemented as planned. Members believe in the group's decision because they've had an active part in examining a problem and determining its solution. Remember:

- Beware of compromises—they mean that not everyone is wholeheartedly behind an idea.

- Reaching consensus guards against later "I told you so" comments from disgruntled teammates.

- Take time for everyone to share perceptions about the problem.

- Ensure that all team members get a chance to share their initial viewpoints before proceeding to identify areas of agreement.

- Encourage all team players to keep a flexible point of view.

- Exchange ideas—this is a great way to learn.

- Keep an open, nondefensive mind.

Chapter Four Review

Answers to these questions appear on page 89.

1. Getting a decision people can live with is called:

   __ A. Consensus
   __ B. Collaboration
   __ C. Commitment
   __ D. Compromise

2. Consensus is the _____ and _____ of the team to an idea or decision.

3. List four consensus skills and describe how to use them.

   _____

   _____

   _____

   _____

4. The story, *The King, The Three Wise People, and the Mysterious Animal,* shows that people can hold _____ views about the same thing.

5. True/False. The process of achieving consensus involves getting people with different points of view to start seeing things in a similar way.

6. True/False. One way to help your team build consensus skills is to work together on a non-work-related problem.

Chapter Five

Learning to Manage Conflict

Chapter Objectives

After completing this chapter, you should be able to:

- Identify four typical sources of conflict in work teams.

- Describe five methods for dealing with conflicting ideas and approaches.

- Identify things to do to build trust among team members so that conflict becomes an asset, not a destructive force.

Conflict

Conflict. The word conjures up images for everyone. What do you think of when you think of the word conflict? Write three images that come to mind:

_____

_____

_____

Let's examine this topic a little more closely. Conflict. Say you're in a team meeting, presenting your ideas. You think you've been pretty smart, even brilliant. Then someone says, "I don't agree. I don't think we should do that at all. In fact, we ought to do it this way." How do you feel? Write what best describes your feelings at that moment:

_____

_____

_____

_____

There's No Escaping Conflict

Conflict touches everyone. There is no escaping it. As you probably indicated, conflict is usually not a positive experience. It isn't for most people. In fact, conflict makes some people so uncomfortable that they would do anything to avoid it. That's because conflict between people often makes its appearance through angry words, pounding fists, emotional and loud voices, hurt feelings, withdrawal, and even confusion. Ideas stop flowing, people stop talking, things stop happening.

It doesn't have to be that way. In teams, conflict comes with the territory. Whenever a diverse group of people comes together to work as a team, their ideas about how to get things done are going to be different. There will be conflict. Successful team members recognize the value of bringing different opinions to the table and managing the resulting conflict.

> **Conflict becomes an opportunity . . . it energizes work.**

Instead of stirring up anger and emotion, conflict becomes an opportunity. When teams understand how to make conflict an opportunity, conflict doesn't stop work. Instead, it actually energizes work. As you'll see, it takes cooperation and trust among team members to harness that energy and put conflict to work.

Avoiding Unnecessary Conflict

Effective team members are not afraid of conflict arising among team members. Some team conflicts are valuable. In fact, conflicting ideas forge higher-quality outcomes. On the other hand, every team should be wary of unnecessary conflict. Unnecessary conflict gets in the way of the team's work.

Look at the following list of the typical sources of conflict for a team. Identify which sources might be valuable and which ones are unnecessary. Then suggest how to avoid an unnecessary source of conflict.

Typical Source of Conflict	Valuable or Unnecessary?	How to Avoid When Unnecessary
1. Goals and rewards differ among team members. Self-interest predominates.		
2. Members view the organization from their own functional view (e.g., treatment, operations, security, training without seeing the big picture).		
3. Members haven't been told to cooperate, or they believe that the team is a chance for them to win while others lose.		
4. New members join the team late and bring up ideas already addressed by the team.		
5. Members think they are right because they have facts or experience other team members don't have.		
6. Members like to test ideas by challenging decisions and authority.		
7. Some members have values and beliefs about work that sometimes are contrary to the group.		

Let's take a closer look at each one.

Goals and Rewards Are Different

Unfortunately, many teams are formed by individuals whose "real" work is not the team's work. One of the fundamental and defining traits of a team—a common goal and benefits for all—is missing. This source of conflict is unnecessary. Team members, even those from different parts of an organization, should be accountable for their team work and should be rewarded for its success. Team rewards are common in many organizations that empower groups of workers. These issues may be addressed through the team code of conduct.

Functional Views of the Organization Prevail

You might say it is valuable to have differing views around the table. However, if there is not a shared view of how all the pieces of the organization fit together as a system, the resulting conflict can be unproductive. Too often, different functions within an organization come to a team to represent their own interests. A team can avoid this unnecessary conflict by developing a systems diagram—a map—of how each function contributes and is linked to accomplishing the mission and goals. For example, suppose a facility's mission includes maintaining security or keeping the public safe and fostering change in offenders' behavior. Programs cannot exist without good security practices. Similarly, good programs help create a calmer environment by helping offenders improve their behavior and keeping them occupied. The systems map would show the link between these two areas and how they benefit the facility. Creating and committing to a systems diagram is an im-

> Develop a systems diagram—a map—to show how functions contribute and link to the mission and goals.

portant ground rule to establish before the team's work can be effective.

People Want to Win

Long-established rivalries among people, departments, and locations can cause members to arrive at team meetings with concerns. For example, a member may be concerned that other members may gain something—extra resources, power, prestige, access to higher levels—at his or her expense. As a result, team meetings run into unnecessary roadblocks. Politics is a reality in correctional organizations. A well-thought-out team code of conduct may go a long way in breaking down these barriers.

New Members Join the Team Late

New members should be briefed and thoroughly oriented to the team, its goals, the team code of conduct, the history of its achievements, its strengths, and its future plans. New members also can be assigned a mentor to help in their orientation process. This way, unnecessary conflict can be avoided. On the other hand, revisiting ideas through the naive questions and ideas of new members may be a valuable way to review how decisions were made. New members may even contribute a fresh perspective and surprising insights into problems the group thought it had addressed completely. Decide how you will handle this situation in your team code of conduct.

Members Think They Are Right

Facts and experience are the currency of team meetings. Conflicts based on different facts and different views of facts are extremely valuable. Conflicts based on experience and data can be researched, validated, verified, reinterpreted, and discussed until common ground is identified. Team collaboration and consensus skills apply here.

Members Like to Test Ideas

This is the gadfly phenomenon, and many teams have at least one. Although he or she may be annoying, the gadfly is another important and valuable source of conflict. Challenges, contrary views, naysaying, and off-the-wall hypothetical examples offer an opportunity to thoroughly examine the consequences of a decision. People who ask penetrating questions that seem to go against the grain of the consensus are serving a purpose. These individuals and their questions should be brought into the process. Team collaboration and consensus skills also apply here.

Some Members Have Different Values and Beliefs

Like the gadfly, members with different values and beliefs force the team to look hard at their decisions. For example, a decision involving flexible work hours might not be valid— unless a member brought family issues to the team table. Or a team deciding on promotion criteria may not have considered all aspects of the decision—until they have incorporated the views of a newly hired staff member looking to establish a career. Different views, even nonconformist views, are vital to teams. If such views are not presented at the team meeting, they should be actively sought.

Five Ways to Resolve Conflict

Try these different methods when a healthy conflict of ideas and opinions challenges the team. The methods are:

- Bargaining
- Problem Solving
- Voting
- Research
- Third-party mediation

Let's take a closer look at each of these five methods:

Bargaining

This is a method most people are familiar with. Bargaining is simply a matter of "If you do this, I'll do that." Call it horse trading, basic politicking, dealing, or negotiating. Bargaining usually resolves conflicts through compromise.

How to Do It

- Before you start bargaining, identify what your bargaining chips are, that is, what you're willing to give up.

- See if you can do the same thing for the other side. Speculate on what their bargaining chips are.

- At the same time, decide your absolute minimum acceptable resolution, the limit of bargain beyond which you simply cannot go.

- Start the process by presenting the least valuable of your bargaining chips. Offer it ("If you do this, I'll do that") and see what happens.

Think through these questions and then write down your responses:

What types of conflict in your team can be effectively handled by bargaining?

_____

_____

_____

_____

_____

_____

Why would bargaining help conflict resolution in your team?

_____

_____

_____

_____

_____

_____

Why would it hinder conflict resolution?

_____

_____

_____

_____

_____

_____

_____

Problem Solving

This is one of the most objective ways of dealing with conflict. The key is to get different sides to define the real problem everyone is trying to solve. Once the problem is clear, the team can apply team collaboration skills to develop alternatives. Identifying the problem may highlight misunderstandings within the group that can be cleared up.

How to Do It

- Make sure that everyone involved in the conflict participates in the problem-solving process.

- Restate the goal of the team in trying to resolve the conflict. "Remember, our purpose is to raise money for the staff sunshine drive as quickly as possible."

- Ask each side of the conflict to present its view. Probe for facts that have led to those points of view and avoid arguing.

- As a result of hearing these different views, state the problem. "We have two different opinions about how to ask the staff for money. One is direct and demanding, requiring a specific amount; the other is more open-ended. Is that our problem?"

- Develop alternatives, using team collaboration skills. Be creative and encourage all members to participate.

- Evaluate the alternatives and select one that works for everyone.

Think through these questions and then write down your responses:

Problem solving is probably one of the most effective methods for teams to use in resolving conflict. Can you identify a current conflict or anticipate a future conflict that can benefit from a problem-solving approach?

_____

_____

_____

_____

_____

Why does clearly identifying the problem sometimes provide an immediate resolution to the conflict?

_____

_____

_____

_____

_____

Voting

Yes, simply voting for one side or the other is a legitimate way to resolve conflict. It's the parliamentary approach. Of course, there are winners and losers in a voting situation, so there are some distinct disadvantages. A vote resolution to a conflict may have even less support than a compromise. Special care should be given to selecting which conflicts are appropriate for resolution through voting.

How to Do It

- Ask the team whether it thinks the conflict should be voted on. Discuss the consequences.

- State the problem as a yes-or-no question. For example, "Should we request overtime for each member of the team?"

- Ask for a vote and count the yeas and nays. Your team may decide a two-thirds majority is necessary or simply a majority.

- If necessary, ask how winners and losers feel.

Think through these questions and then write down your responses:

Has your team ever voted on a conflict? What were the consequences?

_____

_____

_____

_____

How would you recommend the team do it differently, if it had the chance?

_____

_____

_____

_____

If you haven't voted on a conflict, what would be a likely conflict to vote on? What are the risks and advantages of voting?

_____

_____

_____

_____

Research

Start with the research question.

Many teams argue about issues on the basis of lots of opinions and few hard facts. One objective way to resolve these endless discussions is to gather data through research and interpret the findings. If the findings are inconclusive, then either conduct more research or accept the ambiguity and start problem solving.

How to Do It

- Before conducting research, define the fundamental question that needs to be answered to resolve the conflict. This is called the research question.

- Select an appropriate method. There are many different types of research:
  —Conduct focus groups: Ask other teams or groups what they think.
  —Review documented records: Examine and analyze historical data.

—Interview different people: Ask questions, gather other opinions.

—Experiment: Collect data on an existing process, analyze it, and draw conclusions.

—Conduct a survey or questionnaire: Reach a larger group through paper-based methods. Or, if your organization has a networked computer, use E-mail.

Think through these questions and then write down your responses:

Under what circumstances should your team conduct research to resolve a conflict?

_____

_____

_____

What resources do you need inside and outside your team to help you do the research?

_____

_____

_____

_____

Would the results be available in time to affect the team?

_____

_____

_____

_____

What happens if members disagree on the

interpretation of the findings?

_____

_____

_____

_____

Third-Party Mediation

When conflicts within the team reach a point of inflexibility, the time may be right to seek the counsel of an objective third party. Objectivity is key. If the mediator appears biased, either toward one team member or a particular point of view, the process is undermined. For this reason, the team should be particularly wary of going to a direct supervisor or manager to break a deadlock.

Be wary of going to a direct supervisor or manager to break a deadlock.

How to Do It

- The team should identify who the objective third-party mediator should be.

- Before the mediation process, all parties must agree to abide by the results.

- During mediation, each side will present its facts and opinions. The mediator will ask questions.

- A good mediator will try to facilitate problem solving among the conflicting parties. Only when this fails to reach a breakthrough will the mediator make a final determination.

- The team should reflect on the process, seeking to learn how to avoid the inflexibility that led to mediation instead of a team-generated resolution.

Think through these questions and then write down your responses:

What are some of the benefits of mediation?

_____

_____

_____

_____

What are the risks?

_____

_____

_____

Who would be a good mediator for any conflicts within your team?

_____

How can you tell when it's time to seek a third party?

_____

_____

Why is mediation a last resort?

_____

_____

Trust Makes Conflict Work

Why is trust so critical? The level of trust among team members affects how ideas are generated, how decisions are made, and how conflicts are resolved.

All members must act in a way that fosters trust.

When team members trust each other, the

inevitable and expected conflict among team members becomes an opportunity to foster new thinking and creative ideas. Without trust, conflict can disable a team's progress toward its goals.

Think for a moment of a situation in which a team member or staff person lost your trust. What happened to your working relationship?

_____

_____

_____

_____

As you have learned from experience, when trust between people is lost, it affects how they work together. In the absence of trust, members withhold information, guard their comments, exclude people from discussions, and resist conflict resolution. Trust is extremely difficult to regain.

To effectively manage conflict, as well as do all the other things teams do, all members must act in a way that fosters trust.

How do you build trust? Think of someone you really trust. What is it about that person that leads you to trust him/her (for example, keeps promises, treats people fairly, is honest and straightforward)?

_____

_____

_____

_____

_____

Trust Builders

Team members build trust by how they act both in team meetings and in other settings. Check off the trust builders that are important to you. Remember, these actions work together to build trust.

☐ Consistently meet commitments: Do what you promised to do. Walk the talk.

☐ Bring reliable information to the team: You can build trust when what you are talking about is accurate and based on experience and data.

☐ Demonstrate skill at whatever it is you do. Team members tend to trust people who are competent.

☐ Show a sincere interest in the views, talents, and involvement of other team members. One of the qualities of a team is the blending of unique talents. People trust team members who show an interest in them.

☐ Make balanced judgments that attempt to account for the differences among the team. As the team matures and grows used to working together, individuals seem to drop extreme viewpoints and think almost as a group.

☐ Support the team and its decisions to others. Team members earn the trust of others when they defend, explain, and otherwise endorse the work of the team when it is challenged by others. To do otherwise—by bad-mouthing or second-guessing—undermines the team.

Trust Self-Assessment

To what extent do team members trust you? You can get a rough view of how others trust you by completing this self-assessment from the point of view of another team member. Pick someone with whom you may have had a conflict. See how his or her perception of you may get in the way of having a healthy discussion about conflicting views.

Do you:	Never	Not Usually	Some-times	Most of the Time	Always
1. Consistently meet commitments?	1	2	3	4	5
2. Bring reliable information?	1	2	3	4	5
3. Demonstrate skill?	1	2	3	4	5
4. Show a sincere interest in others?	1	2	3	4	5
5. Make balanced judgments?	1	2	3	4	5
6. Support the team?	1	2	3	4	5

Were you frank and honest in your self-assessment? Are any ratings "sometimes," "not usually," or "never" in the eyes of your team? If so, identify how you can earn an "always" or "most of the time" rating on those that need improvement.

_____

_____

_____

_____

_____

List four actions you can take to boost your "most of the time" rating(s).

_____

_____

_____

_____

Summary

In this chapter, you learned how to manage conflict within your team. Conflict is natural and can be used as an opportunity to energize work. The key to managing conflict in a team is to have productive discussions. Trust makes conflict productive. Therefore, be sure to develop trust among team members so that conflict can lead to something productive—even greater cooperation. Also, be sure to:

- Manage conflict toward productive discussion, not arguments.

- Avoid unnecessary conflict by using your team code of conduct.

- Clarify rules and procedures.

Chapter Five Review

Answers to these questions appear on page 91.

1. True/False. Conflict can be an opportunity for teams and can actually energize work.

2. True/False. People who ask penetrating questions that seem to go against the grain of the team consensus should be removed from the team immediately.

3. List three ways to resolve conflict.

   _____

   _____

   _____

4. When team members _____ each other, the inevitable and expected conflict among them becomes an opportunity to foster new opportunities and creative ideas.

5. List three trust builders.

   _____

   _____

   _____

6. A _____ shows how each function contributes and is linked to accomplishing the mission and goals of a team.

7. Different _____ are vital to teams.

Chapter Six

Relax—You'll Love Your New Identity

Chapter Objectives

After completing this chapter, you should be able to:

- Assess how comfortable you are with the team taking over or participating in traditional management tasks.

- Identify the management tasks your team can begin to take on immediately and those that need to wait for the team to develop additional skills and capabilities.

- Devise a task-focused plan to develop team skills and gradually involve the team in more management activities.

Ode to Team Supervisors/Managers, with Sympathy:
(Demoted from Chief to Couch Potato)

Once you were a supervisor/manager, with a clipboard, a radio and perhaps a door.
Not too long ago, people waited for you to tell them the score.
You were responsible, all-knowing, accountable.
If you said, "Make these changes," that request was insurmountable.
If you said, "Bill, work with Sally this afternoon."
Bill worked with Sally, and none too soon.
The director, an expert, you were the chief.
Your command and control were beyond belief.
You knew, they knew, who you were.
And, oh, how the unit did purr.
Now you're a facilitator, but your team doesn't invite you to talk.
It was hard, it was traumatic when they told you to take a walk.
You have to influence, advise, and empower.
You have to support and have vision by the hour.

And you need soothing reassurance you'll not fail.
Will the numbers be correct? Will the climate re-
main calm?
Will someone find out I'm not useful at all?
You're just a couch potato waiting for a team call.

Changing Role of the Supervisor/Manager

If you're a supervisor or manager in an organization where teams, participatory management, and empowerment are finding a place in your work unit, you may be having an identity crisis. Things may not be as bad as they are for the supervisor/manager in the poem, but you may be questioning your role. Changing how decisions are made, how work improvements are implemented, and all the other things you used to do by yourself creates a sense of discomfort. After all, aren't you responsible and accountable for the performance of the work team?

So far, this workbook has focused on how to be an effective team player. All of the team skills apply to you. After all, you are a team player both in a cross-functional supervision/management team and in your own work-unit team. This chapter is devoted to the correctional supervisor's or manager's changing role in the culture shift to a team-oriented environment. This chapter will show you a systematic way of looking at your role in relation to team activities. And, it will give you some guidelines for being the supervisor or manager of an empowered work team.

First, let's find out what your comfort level is with involving teams in traditional supervision or management activities.

Comfort-Level Rating Scale

My comfort level for involving team members:	Very Low	Low	Moderate	High	Very High
1. Establishing direction and priorities	1	2	3	4	5
2. Deciding what to do in the work unit	1	2	3	4	5
3. Deciding how to do it	1	2	3	4	5
4. Planning next steps	1	2	3	4	5
5. Monitoring/checking progress	1	2	3	4	5
6. Deciding on corrective action	1	2	3	4	5
7. Providing rewards and recognition	1	2	3	4	5

In the space below, list the areas where you are most and least comfortable in involving the team.

Most comfortable

_____

_____

_____

_____

_____

Least comfortable

_____

_____

_____

_____

_____

Transitioning to Team Leader

As a supervisor or manager of a team-oriented work unit, you are still accountable for results. So, how do you confront the challenge of developing empowered teams? The best advice for you to follow is to first recognize where you feel comfortable and where you have discomfort. Then, develop a way to help the team evolve. Here's a three-step approach.

1.   Identify opportunities for involving the team where you feel comfortable.

2.   Develop team members' skills.

3.   Gradually add responsibilities as the team's capabilities grow.

No, you do not have to turn over the keys of the organization to the team. The process of developing the team should be evolutionary, not revolutionary. Now, does that make you feel more comfortable? No? Let's take a closer look at how to develop the team.

Look at the following table. Down the left side are the supervision/management tasks traditionally done by you, the supervisor or manager. Across the top are examples of how different groups typically reassign these supervision/management tasks. At the task intersections, a "T" indicates what the team does and has responsibility for. A "Y" shows what you, the supervisor or manager, do. Self-directed work teams, for example, do most of the tasks associated with running their work unit. However, establishing direction and priorities are most likely a supervision/management task. You decide what your team should get involved in and when. See, you really do have some control here.

Take a moment to identify what kinds of supervision/management tasks your team can become involved in doing right now. Mark them with an "R" for "right now." Then, indicate the tasks the team can do with some development and those which the team is not likely to be doing in the future—either because of your personal comfort level or the culture of the organization. Mark those tasks with a "D" for "Development" or an "N" for "Not now."

You're on your way to creating a task-based plan for phasing over different supervision/management roles to the team. This plan, by the way, is under your control. Now that should make you feel even better.

Key:	**T** = team responsibility	**R** = right now
	M = manager responsibility	**D** = development
		N = not now

Representative Task	Self-Directed Team	Staff Involved Team	Supervisor/ Manager Led Team	Your Team
Establish direction and priorities	Y or T	Y	Y	
Decide what to do in the work unit	T	T	Y	
Decide how to do it	T	T	T	
Plan next steps	T	Y and T	Y and T	
Monitor/check progress	T	T	Y	
Provide rewards and recognition	T	Y	Y	

After you've completed the chart, work out your plan. In developing team members, think of the team skills—code of conduct, collaboration, consensus, cooperation—that you feel are most appropriate to the supervision/management task.

In completing the planning form:

- List those supervision/management tasks you can ask the team to do now.

- Identify those supervision/management tasks that the team can become involved in with some skill development and coaching.

- Specify the team skills to help that development.

- Estimate the date when the team can expect to give the task a trial.

- List those skills that you want to reserve for yourself or your supervisor, at least for now.

	Team Skill(s) to Focus on*	Date of Implementation Trial
Tasks Team Can Do Right Now		
Tasks to Develop		
Tasks for Later Consideration		

*Team skills: code of conduct, collaboration, consensus, and cooperation.

Guidelines for Supervisors and Managers of Empowered Work Teams

Here's some advice gathered from supervisors/managers like you, who are dealing with the shift to an empowered team environment.

First, focus on your priorities as a team manager.

1. Get clear on the organization's mission and goals; decide how to translate this direction into priorities and goals for your work unit.

2. Establish performance standards based on the expectations of your organization. After initial standards are created, the team can use them as a benchmark to start its process-improvement efforts.

3. Develop the team's capabilities, specifying what the team is empowered to do today and the skills it needs to develop in order to add other tasks in the future.

4. Ensure that individual team members have the work skills to do their jobs today and prepare them for new job skills for tomorrow.

Second, become an excellent team facilitator and coach.

1. Steer team meetings, don't drive them. The key here is asking for contributions as you go along. For instance, instead of giving orders ("We're going to move the inmates to the new wing, and here's how we're going to do it."), give members a chance to contribute ("We're going to move the inmates to the new wing. Any ideas on how we can do that safely, quickly, and without disrupting the normal schedule?").

2. Let the team talk without saying, "Yes, but..." Don't edit what people say in team meetings; don't cut them off. Allow discussion to happen.

Be sure to *steer* team meetings.

3. On the other hand, learn how to control discussions. Don't allow rambling and repetition. Move the team through the issues to a definite conclusion. When the team makes decisions, ensure that the members know what criteria are to be considered in making a choice—that is, expenses, resources, time, and so forth.

Breaking dependency on the supervisor or manager is one important step in creating empowered teams.

4. Frequently remind the team who the ultimate beneficiaries of the work are. Refocusing on the organization's chart or constituents is often a way of making priorities clear for the team.

5. Don't make decisions that the team should make for itself. Learn to push appropriate decisions down. Breaking dependency on the supervisor or manager is an important step in creating empowered teams.

6. Finally, be a cheerleader. Learn to say, "Yea!" and "Sure, let's try it and see what happens," and "Yes."

Finally, learn to be an effective team player yourself.

1. Team members will expect you to practice what you preach. Learn the team skills presented in this workbook, as well as others not addressed. As a supervisor or manager, you are already a team member of different supervision/management and cross-functional teams. If you play your cards right, your team might let you be a part-time member, instead of just a leader.

2. Define your own role as team player. Hint: Supervisors and managers make great resource-gatherers and messengers to higher levels.

3. Try to adjust. Teams are really good for you
    and the organization.

Benefits to the Supervisor or Manager

What are the benefits to you, the supervisor/manager, when you make the changes needed to shift to an empowered team environment? Supervisors and managers remain responsible and accountable for results. But in a team environment, the team shares the responsibility. A major benefit of involving teams and empowering staff is that you don't have to do it all by yourself.

> **In a team environment, you don't have to do it all by yourself.**

Teams create a surprising sense of energy and enthusiasm in the workplace. If you nurture this energy and keep it focused on the work, members will be happier and results will startle even you. In fact, productivity and quality will go up. Morale goes up, too. Research shows that's what happens when teams share responsibility for getting things done.

Finally, the quality of work life will be better. Guiding, developing, and leading people is more rewarding in the long run than dispensing orders on a routine basis, though there is a necessary time and place for orders in the correctional environment. You still have responsibilities and accountabilities. But your stress level will probably go down, your evenings and weekends will be family time again, and you'll feel closer to your team members and colleagues.

Summary

For many correctional supervisors and managers, making the transition to a team environment can be distressing. But making the switch to empowered teams can be seen as a process controlled by the supervisor or manager, not a process with a life of its own. Remember that a shift in your role doesn't mean that you are no longer important.

- Goals still need to be met.

- People and teams still need direction.

- Resources and development are still crucial.

Supervisors and managers can learn to turn over some activities to the team and retain other responsibilities. The benefits of a well-functioning team far exceed any liabilities. Many supervisors and managers believe that teams:

- Get the best work done.

- Ensure quality products and services.

- Keep staff, offenders, the public—all constituents or stakeholders (all those affected by a decision)—happy or satisfied.

Chapter Six Review

Answers to these questions appear on page 92.

1. List the three steps for helping a team evolve and take on greater responsibilities.

   _____

   _____

   _____

2. What is the first step to dealing with the challenges of developing an empowered team?

   _____

3. List two ways that you can focus on your priorities as a Team Manager.

   _____

   _____

4. To be a good facilitator or coach, you should:

   - _____team meetings, don't _____ them.
   - Let the team talk without _____.
   - Frequently remind the team who the ultimate _____ of the work are.
   - Learn how to _____ discussions.
   - Don't make _____ the team should make for itself.
   - Be a _____ for the team.

5. List two ways that you can be an effective team player.

   _____

   _____

6. Identify four benefits of having empowered teams in the correctional environment.

   _____

   _____

   _____

   _____

Post-Test

Assess your understanding of how to be an effective team player by answering the following questions:

1. The three traits of a team are shared purpose, people having to _____ _____, and benefits for everyone.

2. After defining its goals, a new team should spend time writing the team _____.

3. Laughter is an indicator that the team skill of _____ is being used effectively to solve a problem.

4. When a team is reaching a decision, a _____ is preferred over a compromise.

5. If team members can manage it, _____ can actually contribute to better decisions.

6. If team members don't arrive at meetings on time, the team should examine the team _____.

7. Announcements, progress reports, problem solving, decision making, and planning are common team meeting _____.

8. Team members have achieved a _____ when individuals feel committed to a decision.

9. Anyone _____ can become involved in the team collaboration process that results in a creative solution.

10. A _____ is anyone who is affected by the decisions of a team and should have a say in deciding the final outcome.

See page 94 for answers.

Answers to Chapter Reviews

Chapter One Review

1. Benefits of working in teams are:
   - Accomplishing more on the job with less waste of time and materials
   - Producing higher-quality work
   - Being happier with your job
   - Managing offenders more effectively

2. Teams have these traits in common:
   - Share a **purpose** or **common** goal
   - People **work** together
   - A **benefit** for everyone on the team

3. The four C's of team player skills are:
   - Code of Conduct
   - Team Collaboration
   - Team Consensus
   - Team Cooperation

4. **False.** On a team, no one "wins" an argument.

5. **True.**

Chapter Two Review

1. A code of conduct is a document that establishes operating principles, policies, and ground rules that everyone on the team learns, understands, and is willing to comply with.

2. Two benefits of a code of conduct are:
   - Clears doubts about what will happen on the team.
   - Creates a positive, specific framework that describes how the team will work.

3. The future-forward method of writing a code of conduct begins with imagining the future success of the team. Then, the team works backward, deciding what it took to get there.

4. The "anticipating predictable problems" method of writing a code of conduct is to examine the list of predictable and frequent problems teams can expect. Then, team members generate ideas to avoid these problems.

5. You can influence your team's code of conduct by:
   - Asking **other teams** how they manage their process,
   - Not being **shy or reluctant to speak**,
   - Asking the team to **review** the code of conduct from time to time,
   - Reviewing the code of conduct before **critical meetings** that require consensus or collaboration, and
   - Asking the team to form a committee whose goal is to **monitor compliance** with the code of conduct.

Chapter Three Review

1. Collaboration is solving a problem as a group.

2. Collaboration is slowed down by team members':
   A. Hidden agendas
   B. Anger
   C. Personality traits
   √ D. Fear

3. **True.**

4. Three of the ways to help bring creative ideas to the table are:
   - Listening with interest and respect to what members say.
   - Encouraging people to ask "what if" questions.
   - Allowing time for thinking.

5. Ways to improve team collaboration skills are:
   - Conduct creative warm-up exercises at every team meeting.
   - Practice, practice, practice.
   - Post team collaboration skills on the wall and review them before the next meeting.
   - Allow time for ideas to happen.
   - Suggest that your team visit other teams that are good at collaboration skills.
   - Get an outside facilitator to attend your meetings.
   - Ask your team to practice "ambiance engineering."
   - Study the problem.
   - Celebrate an exciting and productive team meeting with a fun event outside of work.
   - Think of some respected and credible figure in your organization or the criminal justice field—a person who has a good reputation for creativity, ideas, and uniqueness. Ask the team to think about how that person would address the problem.

Chapter Four Review

1. Getting a decision people can live with is called:
   - √   A. Consensus
   - B. Collaboration
   - C. Commitment
   - D. Compromise

2. Consensus is the **agreement** and **commitment** of the team to an idea or decision.

3. Consensus skills include:

- Ask each individual how he or she feels about the situation. Go around the table and give everyone a chance to say something.
- Ask for facts, definitions, or explanations, and try to uncover what different thoughts or words really mean to team members. Ask members to explain their views. Be sure that members focus on words.
- Clarify discrepancies of opinions with facts. Make sure to get the facts on the table. If members cannot support their opinions with facts, get more data before continuing.
- Modify your views when faced with compelling facts. Test and weigh the prevailing facts, try on the other persons' views and see whether they're acceptable to you.
- Identify similarities and differences among the points of view on the team. Discuss similarities and crystallize the differences in a single statement.
- Reinforce open-mindedness and the need for cooperation. Refer to the team code of conduct to ensure open discussion.
- Remain nondefensive when challenged and avoid emotional encounters. Stay silent when you're being criticized and let the person finish before you respond. Be empathic with the person's point of view.
- List the positive and negative aspects or consequences of each point of view. Weigh each viewpoint carefully, exploring the associated risks.

- Be sure that each team member participates. Go around the table and ask each person to speak.
- Through discussion, define the risk level associated with a decision that is not working and develop an approach that minimizes that risk for everyone. Assess the risks of each decision and discuss them thoroughly.

4. The story, *The King, The Three Wise People, and the Mysterious Animal*, shows that people can hold **different** views about the same thing.

5. **True.**

6. **True.**

Chapter Five Review

1. **True.**

2. **False.** These people should stay on the team because they serve a purpose. Their opinions encourage team members to thoroughly examine the consequences of a decision.

3. Ways to resolve conflict are:
- Bargaining
- Problem solving
- Voting
- Research
- Third-party mediation

4. When team members trust each other, the inevitable and expected conflict among them becomes an opportunity to foster new opportunities and creative ideas.

5. Ways to build trust include:
    *   Consistently meet commitments.
    *   Bring reliable information to the team.
    *   Demonstrate skill at whatever it is you do.
    *   Show a sincere interest in the views, talents, and involvement of other team members.
    *   Make balanced judgments that attempt to account for the differences among the team.
    *   Support the team and its decisions to others.

6. A **systems diagram** shows how each function contributes and is linked to accomplishing the mission and goals of a team.

7. Different **views (or opinions or ideas)** are vital to teams.

Chapter Six Review

1. The three steps for helping a team evolve and take on greater responsibilities are:
    *   Identify opportunities for involving the team where you feel comfortable.
    *   Develop team members' skills.
    *   Gradually add responsibilities as the team's capabilities grow.

2. The first step to dealing with the challenges of developing an empowered team is:

    Recognize where you feel comfortable and where you have discomfort.

3. Ways you can focus on your priorities as a Team Manager include:
    *   Get clear on the organization's mission and goals; decide how to translate this

direction into priorities and goals for your work unit.

- Establish performance standards based on the expectations of your organization.
- Develop the team's capabilities.
- Ensure that individual team members have the work skills to do their jobs today and prepare them for new job skills for tomorrow.

4. To be a good facilitator or coach, you should.
    - **Steer** team meetings; don't **drive** them.
    - Let the team talk without saying, "**Yes, but…**"
    - Frequently remind the team who the ultimate **beneficiaries** of the work are.
    - Learn how to **control** discussions.
    - Don't make **decisions** the team should make for itself.
    - Be a **cheerleader** for the team.

5. Ways you can be an effective team player include:
    - Practice what you preach.
    - Define your own role as a team player.
    - Try to adjust.

6. Benefits of having empowered teams in the correctional environment are:
    - The team shares the responsibility for getting tasks done and achieving goals.
    - Teams create energy and enthusiasm in the workplace.
    - Productivity and quality will go up.
    - Morale will go up.
    - The quality of work life will be better.
    - Your stress level probably will go down.

Post-Test Answers

1. The three traits of a team are shared purpose, people having to **work together**, and benefits for everyone.

2. After defining its goals, a new team should spend time writing the team **code of conduct**.

3. Laughter is an indicator that the team skills of **collaboration** are being used effectively to solve a problem.

4. When a team is reaching a decision, a **consensus** is preferred over a compromise.

5. If team members can manage it, **conflict** can actually contribute to better decisions.

6. If team members don't arrive at meetings on time, the team should examine the team **code of conduct**.

7. Announcements, progress reports, problem solving, decision making, and planning are common team meeting **activities**.

8. Team members have achieved a **consensus** when individuals feel committed to a decision.

9. Anyone **involved with a problem** can become involved in the team collaboration process that results in a creative solution.

10. A **stakeholder** is anyone who is affected by the decisions of a team and should have a say in deciding the final outcome.